Table

Loan Officer Recruiting

How to Effectively Recruit, Hire and Retain Mortgage Production Talent

MICHAEL D. BAKER

Published by

www.MikeBakerOnline.com

(800) 928-7110

ISBN: **9721658-1-9**

Author and Editor:

Michael D. Baker
(800) 928-7110
www.MikeBakerOnline.com

Cover and Interior Design by:

N9 Design
Nartui Gutierrez
info@n9-design.com
www.n9-design.com

About Mike Baker

Michael Dale Baker attended Point Loma College in San Diego and Fresno State University in Fresno, California, with a major in Speech Communication and Business Administration. He is also a graduate of the "The School of Mortgage Banking" through the "Mortgage Bankers Association of America."

Mike Baker is a nationally recognized speaker, author, manager and performance consultant specializing in the mortgage origination industry. He started his career in 1980 and worked his way up to being one of the top loan originators and top managers in the country with his enthusiasm and recruiting abilities. He is passionate about helping loan originators and managers grow their business.

Since 1995, Mike has been sharing his expertise throughout the mortgage industries as a consultant and trainer bringing high energy and motivational wisdom to his numerous speaking engagements. Mike has written numerous monthly articles for *Mortgage Originator Magazine* and other mortgage publications since 1998. In addition, Mike has published two other books, including *Mortgage Power* and *Recruiting Top Mortgage Loan Originators*.

Today, Mike is the President and CEO of The Mortgage Coach in Irvine, California. Formerly an outside endorser of the company, Mike came aboard after embracing the software as a 'must have' for any mortgage originator who desires to achieve the Trusted Advisor status—the mark of a true mortgage banking professional. The Mortgage Coach is the Leader in Mortgage Advisory Software.

"As I was growing up, my father always told me to master a job before I take on additional responsibility. When I entered the mortgage origination industry, I started out as a loan originator. I went from loan originator to sales manager to branch manager to regional manager to vice president of production to becoming self-employed as an author, speaker and trainer. I am passionate about sharing what has worked for me as well as the mistakes and learning experiences that I've had."

Introduction

One of the most important and difficult jobs in the mortgage business is recruiting and hiring talent. Like the produce section of the grocery store, you want to select the best fruits and vegetables available that day. If you have to settle because everything is picked over, then you select the best you can and spend more time cleaning and preparing in order to have the best meal. When you go to the department store to buy a shirt, you find one in your size and then make sure that there are no marks or snags on the one you select. You want the best one available. In sports, who knows who will emerge as a great impact player? Many great players grew to be absolutely awesome, yet were not selected early in the draft or not at all. Many began their careers late in life only to rise to the top in their field. In life, we all want the best that is available at the time. When you think about it, life is pretty simple. If you hire the best, you have a good shot at being the best if you can get the best people working together. If you don't have the best people, your chances of success dramatically decrease. As simple as it sounds, that's the hard part and that's what this book is all about. Proven strategies that work in today's competitive mortgage origination environment.

I set this book up in a way that induces action! In each section, we will be stating an objective, taking an action, and monitoring the process all the way to completion. After all, taking action is the most important part. I didn't just want to write a book just to say I wrote a book. I want managers to really be able to get a great result by following the steps outlined here. We all know that it's not enough just to know how to do something. We must act on our knowledge. This guide will assist you in hiring a great team of performance players.

Now, with all of that said, let's get down to the business of recruiting for an overall win. Not just the short-term wins, but long-term wins as well. This book is designed to help you organize an effective recruiting process to hire talented people. This book was developed specifically to hire talented sales people; however, some of the principles and strategies can be applied to recruiting talented processors, underwriters, funders, receptionists and all other team members as well. This is a practical tool that guides you through the logical steps to recruit great loan originators.So, how do you know how to pick top achievers? How do you know who will emerge to be an impact player for your company? How do you get them to work for you? By using the ideas, strategies and tools in this book, you'll be equipped to answer these and other tough questions when it comes to selecting, recruiting, hiring, and retaining the best!

Let's begin!

Sincerely,
Michael D. Baker

CHAPTER I: The Foundation of Recruiting Success

The first step is to diligently SEEK THEM OUT! Decide what you're looking for. Know what you're looking for and go after it. Make deliberate decisions about who you want working for you. Then track and measure the results you're getting. A lot of people say that hiring is a gamble. No matter what you do, you never really know if someone will work out or not. Let me give you some out-of-the-box examples that can increase your odds of success.

A friend of mine owns several rental properties. He has never had a problem with a tenant. I asked him how he does it? He said, I check to see if their shoes and their car are clean. I greet them, and I know within five minutes if they will be good tenants or not. He said if they take care of their shoes and their car, then chances are they will take care of the house as well. I laughed! However, I also feel that there is wisdom here.Years ago I went to a mortgage banking seminar on recruiting. They recommended having all candidates take several written tests. Tests that would disclose the aptitude, personality, and overall future conduct that the individual taking the test might have. While these types of tests seem prudent, the fact is, most of the time they just don't work. The University of Southern California did a study on this and found that only 15% of the group participants were found to have similarities with their test results. While these testings have their place, nothing will replace good old common sense and some due diligence.

Hire for ATTITUDE and DESIRE and watch everything else fall into place…

I do something a little different. I try to watch the candidate drive up to the office building for our interview. I learn a lot by watching them drive in, get out of their car and head toward the office. Now please don't laugh, just keep reading. Thank you! What I learn by doing this is their level of commitment to what is about to happen. Don't get me wrong, this is not foolproof. This just gives me a feel about how committed this person might be in meeting job requirements, personal performance and company standards. Are they ready for this interview? Are they confident? Do they know what they want? Do they walk with purpose? Are they prepared for this interview? Are they committed? Do they want this job?

How can I tell all of this by watching them get out of their car? For example, if they're late, or if they fiddle around in their car before they get out, if they walk slowly, if they have trouble finding the office, then chances are they are not very serious or excited about this interview or this job. But if they get out of their car, grab their briefcase or notebook, and head straight for the office, that seems to show more direction, more purpose, more of an "I want this job" attitude.

When the candidate gets into the office, you will really be able to notice what I'm talking about. Do they look you in the eye or do their eyes wander? Do they have a firm handshake? Do they have a professional posture and body language? You can tell a lot about a person in the first five minutes. There are many books and tapes on the market that can help you get more knowledgeable on physiological and body language communication. This knowledge and education can save you a lot of time in selecting the right players for your team.

Have you always wondered why some mortgage companies and mortgage branches excel and are extremely successful, while others are mediocre or on the verge of getting closed down? Have you ever wondered why some managers always seem to attract talent? Some managers seem to attract top achievers like a magnet. I believe that the reason for success in any branch or organization is driven by the power (or lack thereof) of the leadership. I always say, "As you go, so goes your organization." If the leadership is positive and cares about customer service, growth, success and improvement, then all those around them will care also. If the leadership doesn't care, then it's difficult to get others to care.

So how does one develop this strong leadership and charisma? The easiest way that I've found is to MODEL WHAT WORKS! For the last ten years, I have been researching, interviewing, studying and seeking out answers to these questions. I have been seeking these answers so that I can utilize the success of others to help me to be more successful in my own mortgage career. By seeking out these answers and applying what I've learned, I have been able to get some awesome results. I've been able to get these results at all levels of my experience, from loan originator to branch manager to senior management levels. By paying close attention to others and modeling what is working for them, you can save lots of time and money. By learning from other people's successes and failures, you can by-pass mistakes and get to where you want to be much quicker. In addition to your own new ideas and strategies, use what successful managers are doing to get the same results that they're getting.

WORK ON YOURSELF FIRST! In addition to modeling what works, the next important factor I learned was to work on myself first. To influence other people, we must first influence ourselves. The more positive breakthroughs you have internally, the more breakthroughs you'll have externally. For example, if you know how to master yourself, then you can master your own life, then you can help others master their lives as well. On the other hand, if you can't master yourself, you'll have a difficult time helping others to master themselves. We must lead ourselves before we can start leading others. Even if you have been successful with this, there is always a new level you can go.

This is where honesty and reality come in, while politics take a back seat. There are far too many leaders in business and politics that have little or no business being there, right? Some individuals get to where they are through a basis of self-leadership, while others use slick rhetoric or politic their way up. Obviously, I'm not much on politics. While there is a place for politics, it should take a back seat to what's real. The most successful managers in the world know how to take charge of their own life first. Let that be you!

I'm asking you to become better. Begin the journey to improve yourself daily. If you want an outstanding result in recruiting and building a great team, start with yourself. Start by mastering your own fears. Start by setting new standards for yourself. Start by increasing your certainty and developing a stronger focus. Start by making some new decisions and commitments about what you're now going to demand from yourself and what you'll no longer accept. Learn more so you can earn more! Take actions every day that moves you closer to your outcome.

NEVER STOP RECRUITING! The top managers are always looking for talent. Consistency rules! Make recruiting an ongoing part of your business. Once you master the art of recruiting, you'll be rewarded accordingly. Master the art of recruiting by mastering the information in this book.

With all of that said, I am very excited about sharing these aspects of recruiting in the mortgage origination industry with you. We must approach this subject not only together, but also in the right state of mind to get the most out of it.

I want to make sure that we all have a belief. A belief that our people, our talents, our attitudes, and our teamwork are all critical to the success of any business or organization. I've read a lot of information on recruiting over the years, and they always tend to direct the recruiting effort toward sales people. In other words, recruit great sales people, and you build a great company. In part, this is true. But it's only one piece of the puzzle we're building. While recruiting a great sales force is a must, I would like to expand this thinking into recruiting great people overall to build a great company overall. We all need great behind-the-scenes people as well as sales people. It's critical to have great support people in order to recruit great sales people. We need each other and we must all work together to reach the outcome we're looking for. It all works together!

Hiring talent is the key. However, you can even expand on that statement. Hiring talent, managing and motivating talent, and getting ordinary people to do extraordinary things are all critical to a manager's success. If you want great sales people, be a great manager! If you're clicking on all cylinders internally, you'll be powerful and effective externally.

We all know that being a great manager is being a great coach. A great coach can take ordinary players and get them to rise above their own talents. I like the quote from coach Pat Riley of the Miami Heat basketball team: "There's no talent in hustle." The ability to hustle and take massive action is the driving force behind all success. Add smart, thought-out decisions, solid plans, and good systems, and you'll be a successful player throughout your career.

The best recruiters in the world lead by example. Work hard on yourself and your own management skills daily. If we work harder on ourselves than we do on our jobs, incredible growth begins to set in. I say all of this because it doesn't matter what you learn about recruiting if you're a jerk to work for. It doesn't matter if you're a great recruiter, if you can't keep the talent you're recruiting. It doesn't matter if you hire a lot of top producers if your existing staff can't provide great service and get the loans through the system. It doesn't matter if you're great at recruiting a sales force if you can't keep the inside staff working with you as well. You can't expect others to grow and get better if you're not getting better yourself.

CHAPTER II: Your Company Culture and The Candidate

OVERVIEW

When seeking existing LOs, we all know that every loan originator is different. Each one has a different geographical area to cover, different Realtors or builders he/she cultivates, different types of loans that he/she closes more frequently than others. So, whether you are recruiting a new sales person or a superstar, you want to consider the real job you are filling and describe the skills or experience you need to get. The more precise you can be in defining your outcome, the more likely you are to fulfill it. Clarity is power! Know what you're looking for. Recruiting goals are like production goals. You are more likely to reach your outcome if you define it up-front.

The better the questions you ask yourself regarding the type of individual you want, the better the answers will be. Ask the right questions, get the right answers. Ask good questions, get good answers. Think about the knowledge you need for low-to-moderate lending patterns in your territory. Think about the community knowledge you'd like a new salesperson to have. Consider whether you have a void in the areas of the city your current staff is covering; can a new person cover that void? Would bi-lingual skills help you in opening new markets or better penetrating current markets? Are you in a growing area? What special loan programs do you have in your area? What specific loan programs do you need that also fit your business model in addition to helping you complete? What type of individual would be best to promote your company and loan programs you offer?

See Chapter XII for sample "Job Descriptions." These job descriptions cover three production jobs including, Loan Officer, Managing Loan Officer, and Sales Manager.

The key is to develop a recruiting plan for every Loan Originator you want to hire. Start by defining the target, and then create a series of steps you will take to achieve the target. Put a timetable to the steps. You will always do the things you give yourself a deadline to do!

"Create your own environment for your own success"

ACTIONS TO TAKE

Define the job content; skills and knowledge candidate must have to be able to do the job well.

Job Content	Knowledge Candidate Should Have
• Develops and maintains effective contact in Realtor/Builder/Broker community.	• Do they know Realtors and/or builders well • Do they know the Realtors and/or builders we don't know • Do they know the geography of this market
• Has monthly production level of at least $500,000 (retail) or $2 million (wholesale) (Or set your own standards based on your mission)	• Do they have documentation to demonstrate production level • Can he/she originate loans without having the lowest rates in the marketplace
• Maintains fundamental working knowledge of mortgage business, e.g., compliance issues, credit issues, underwriting guidelines, appraisal issues, interest rates, etc.	• Does he/she speak knowledgeably about current issues in the mortgage business • Does he/she know the interest rates in current market • Does he/she know appraisers, title company staff, and others in the industry
• Produces quality loans in compliance with company standards, investor guidelines, and government/agency regulations.	• Do they have a proven record of quality sales which can be verified through references and documented
• Takes complete loan applications and handles customer service issues.	• Can they describes application process Do they listen and respond to questions appropriately
• Background	• What business do they come from and how will their skills compliment the mortgage industry.

Define personal skills and abilities candidate should have to be successful in this office:

- Is adaptable and flexible in meeting changing market conditions
- Can make sales calls; can take rejection and keep making calls
- Has good self-image and self-confidence; has a professional appearance and manner
- Can (and has) lived on straight commission
- Can work long and irregular hours
- Maintains good documentation and records
- Has good mathematical skills

Define special needs or special knowledge you may require in your local marketplace:

- Bi-lingual skills
- Low-to-moderate borrowers
- Specialized product knowledge
- Specialized geography
- Familiar with FHA/VA lending

DEVELOP A JOB DESCRIPTION AND PLAN FOR HIRE

☑ Checklist
Define job content
Define Skills
Knowledge and Abilities needed
Define special market needs
Develop target dates and a timetable for each step of the plan
Define job content
Review plan
Monitor the plans progress

CHAPTER III:
Sourcing For Candidates

OVERVIEW

The best way to succeed in accomplishing a goal is to have a clear plan for every step and take massive action to accomplish the plan. The more sources for candidates you develop, the more referrals you will receive; the more referrals, the more candidates you can consider. If you have plenty of candidate choices from which to select, you increase your likelihood of hiring a top-notch salespersons.

Sourcing is a process of identifying as many probable targets from which you can draw candidates. You'll want to create a Rolodex with names of loan officers in the community who might want to work for you and those loan officers whom you want to recruit. The task of "sourcing" is to find people who can give you those names; along with a quick assessment of the quality and quantity of business those people produce.

Your goal in sourcing is to collect information about who potential candidates are and how to contact them. Once you have some basic information, you can begin deciding which candidates you want to try to recruit. Use your sources to verify production levels and prior performance of candidates as you talk to your leads.

It's important that you maintain some sort of recruiting log to track conversations with potential recruits. You can use this recruiting log to keep a record of all the talent in your area. The more information that you have on these prospects, the more you can contact them and keep in touch.

It would be well worth the money to invest in database software such as Act, Goldmine, or other reputable software program for your computer. There are many contact management systems on the market today that would work well for keeping track of your contacts on a consistent basis.

Remember, it's a "numbers" game. The more sources you identify, the more candidates you can identify. The more candidates you identify, the more choices you will have to recruit the best Loan Originators for your office.

It's not merely what you know and whom you know that counts. It's how you communicate what you know that will really make a difference in your results.

ACTIONS TO TAKE

Identify as many sources as you can; create a Rolodex card for every source showing:

(Front of card)

Source Name:
Address:
Phone #:

(Back of card)

Date of Contact:	**Outcome:**

Use a similar card as a recruiting log to keep track of your top candidates.

(Front of card)

Prospect:
Company:
Address:
Phone #:
Referred by:

(Back of card)

Types of Loans:
Estimate of Annual Production:
Special Skills or Knowledge:
Date of Contact:
Referred by:
Status:

In addition to developing your own list of sources, here is a list of sources that will get you started:

- *Mortgage Originator's* Top 200 List (April issue)
- *Broker* Magazine
- MBAA
- Educational Events
- Wholesale Representatives
- Competitor mortgage companies or banks
- Mortgage Insurance companies

- Title and Escrow companies
- Current employees, including originators, processors, underwriter, etc.
- FHA Market Share Book
- Mortgage companies merging or closing
- Mortgage companies changing processing or underwriting locations
- Staff of agencies, e.g., Fannie Mae Affordable Housing, and others
- Competitor mortgage brokers or wholesale lenders
- Local Universities and colleges
- Salespeople from other businesses, i.e., UPS, beverage sales, insurance...

Develop a routine of creating sources from professional or civic meetings you attend:

- Realtor Seminars or Open Houses
- Agency Seminars
- Discussions with borrowers who are denied by you or others
- Church meetings
- Civic group meetings, e.g., Chambers of Commerce
- Local clubs such as Lions, Rotary, etc.
- Develop a script you can use with different groups to find names of potential Loan Originators.

  Samples:

  Neighbor: "This is a great neighborhood, with lots of new people moving in. Any idea who has been helping them to arrange financing?"

  Loan Originator: "Who is your toughest competition?

  Realtors, CPA's, Financial Planners, or builders: "Who are the Loan Originators you most enjoy working with?"

NOTE: These source and prospect cards are an on-going task to top recruiters. Keep your sources and prospects up to date.

☑ Checklist
Develop source Rolodex cards
Develop prospect Rolodex cards

CHAPTER IV: Networking Your Leads

OVERVIEW

Once you have identified your sources for candidates, then you need to work those leads in a systematic and persistent fashion. In networking, there are plenty of comparisons to the loan production process. You've got to be out in the marketplace, talking to Realtors and builders, in order to obtain loan business and close it. Likewise, you've got to be out in the marketplace, networking with all your leads, so that you can hire the best salespeople.

Networking is a routine that you must develop to contact a source or a candidate. You'll want to determine if the source has good information on candidates, and/or if the candidate is worth pursuing. If the candidate is viable, then you want to gather as much information as possible to validate that a face-to-face meeting is worth your time.

Remember that not every candidate you contact may be worth pursuing. You have to determine in advance what criteria are acceptable minimum standards, and you have to get enough information in this early stage to be sure your minimums are covered. Don't waste time if you can't get comfortable with your minimums. If you are in doubt, conduct a short meeting. You also will want to consider how much time and training you'll need to invest in each potential candidate. If you don't have time to train, don't spend too much time tracking down new people.

Also, it is critical that you have a follow-up plan to your networking. You may want to mail the candidate a brochure or marketing plan about you and your company. This will build interest and keep the relationship going.

Sometimes immediate failures can be long-term gains. But only if you keep in touch. The candidate may not come with you now, but by keeping in touch, they may later. Some of the best loan officers I have ever recruited took me over a year to land.

TAKE A LESSON FROM THE CHINESE BAMBOO TREE

"On Teams," by Ron Archer (Irwin Professional Publishing, 1996) has a chapter called "Lessons from the Chinese Bamboo Tree." In part, the passage reads, "Building a great team is a lot like trying to grow the most difficult tree in the world, the Chinese Bamboo tree." A farmer takes a seed, plants it and tends it every day for a year. Then the farmer looks at the soil and still sees nothing: "no sprouts, no signs of life." After four years, the farmer still has nothing to show for his labor. Says Archer's parable: "To the untrained eye he seems to be a fool, but the farmer knows that he will have to get to the third month of the fifth year before this seemingly dormant seed grows into a tree that is 90 feet tall. Five years nothing. Three more months, 90 feet!"

"A journey of a thousand miles must begin with a single step."

—Lao Tzu

ACTIONS TO TAKE

- Plan a specific time every day that you will spend on networking your leads.
- Determine what time of day fits best in your schedule so you will network your leads every day.
- Devote at least on hour to this process every day.
- Keep good, consistent notes of your conversations, so that you can reference the idea you discussed with the candidates you want to pursue; update your recruitment log or Rolodex card after every

conversation.

- Get at least one solid lead from every call.
- Have an "opening line" for the first call to a potential candidate which fits your style and which will hopefully appeal to that person, e.g.: "Are you working twice as hard for half the money?"

"Even if you are not interested in changing jobs now, I always like to meet top professionals in our industry."

"I understand from the Realtors that you do a lot of loans."

- Set minimum standards that a prospect must have before you agree to interview him/her as a formal candidate. Refer to your job description and skills required. Also, write down the minimum standards to keep track of your requirements for this job opening.
- Set up meetings with prospects you think can become candidates in a setting that allows private, but relaxed conversation.
- Over meals or coffee (avoid alcoholic drinks since you may not always have privacy or memory recall)
- Attend a sports event, or participate in one with the prospect
- Conduct a preliminary discussion by asking broad questions; then keep quiet, open your ears to listen.
- Ask about the types of business he/she is doing.
- Ask about the company he/she is currently working for.
- Ask what types of loan products he/she likes to sell; what's moving now; what products he/she wishes the current company had, but doesn't.
- Trade war stories (this describes you as a producing manager, if appli cable; you can also tell them your production numbers as a way to obtain his/her production numbers).
- Ask how he/she got into the business? If applicable, ask how he/she has survived the post-refi time.

NOTE: Script the conversation so that you know what information you want to get and ask questions to get it.

What information do I want?	What question to ask to get information?

☑ Checklist
Time each day I will dedicate to networking calls
Develop prospect Rolodex cards
Create note sheet for calls to candidates
Script for this candidate meeting (fill in for each candidate)
Create list of minimum standards each candidate must have

CHAPTER V: Interviewing and Evaluating the Candidate

OVERVIEW

Now you have identified a viable prospect that you can turn into a strong Loan Originator candidate. You've found a candidate who appears to have the right background, qualifications, experience, skills, and production levels. It's time to interview and evaluate the candidate to be sure that what you've seen so far is really what you'll get, if you decide to make the offer to hire.

Your first conversations, or even your first meeting, will have established some mutual interest. Your task in the interview is to get specific facts to back-up the claims of "million-dollar-a-month production," or "great relationships with Realtors," or "I know this market backwards and forwards," or "I have a consumer direct system that will make both of us tons of money."

All of us have been interviewed at some point, and most of us have conducted interviews. Asking the questions is not the tough part of an interview; evaluating the answers is the challenge. You've probably already formed a positive impression about a candidate, if you're willing to spend time doing an interview. Your task now is to get beyond the social niceties and to ask tough, penetrating questions that will help you decide if you want to work with this candidate.

Remember that a large part of your success as a manager depends on the stability, persistence, reliability and knowledge of the sales people in your organization. You need to be sure that this candidate is someone who will work compatibly with other people in the branch, who can operate in our system, who can sell our products at our prices and create good, consistent production levels. Remember, it's more important to hire someone who understands his/her particular role and fits well on your team. Merely landing a top performer is only part of this equation. No matter how much production they do, if they don't fit, they could cause you and your company lots of problems.

The best interviews are the ones in which you do the least talking. Save your "sales pitch" for the end of the interview. You will then be able to sell your branch and/or company to the issues the candidate has told you are his/her reasons to consider leaving the present company.

Once you've completed your interview, make notes of your discussion so that you will recall the answers to your factual questions. This practice is especially important if you are interviewing several candidates for the same opening. Don't record a lot of impressions or qualitative information, but be sure you can keep track of the facts in each candidate's history, e.g. production levels, product lines sold, experience with government loans and so on.

"Read between the lines and apply some due diligence for maximum success in hiring"

ACTIONS TO TAKE

Set interview appointment in a professional location in which interruptions will be at an absolute minimum.

- Use your office or conference room, if candidate is comfortable coming to your office.
- Use a quiet restaurant.
- Do not go to a bar or other social setting; this is a serious conversation and should be treated respectfully.
- If a candidate comes to your office, be sure the receptionist welcomes the candidate, offers coffee, etc. Be sure that the office staff does not interrupt you during the interview.
- Prepare a list of questions you want to ask this candidate which will get you the information you need to evaluate him/her; questions will fall into four basic categories:

  NOTE: See Chapter VI for sample questions

BUSINESS EXPERIENCE
▪ Dates of employment
▪ Company names
▪ Jobs held
▪ Reasons for changing companies
▪ Any time gaps in experience; explain

MORTGAGE BUSINESS KNOWLEDGE
▪ Types of products sold
▪ And sales techniques
▪ Realtor/broker/builder contacts
▪ And compliance knowledge

PRODUCTION LEVELS
▪ Annual production for last calendar year and/or last twelve months
▪ Annual production pre-refinance period
▪ percent of business which is new vs. refinance vs. brokered

PERSONAL QUALIFICATIONS
▪ Sales style
▪ Administrative ability, attention to detail
▪ Professional manner, appearance
▪ Compatibility with you and other staff in branch

- Make sure that you stay "legal" in asking your questions (*see* Chapter VI and XI).
- Plan to invest at least one hour conducting the interview.
- Have your candidates meet with other staff members in the company.
- It's good to have another opinion to verify your impressions, either good or bad.

It's also important to have a read from your office manager or other branch leader on how this candidate will work with the support staff.

You may also get some helpful information by having the candidate talk with one of your current sales people. The candidate may also want to interview one of your sales people to verify some of the information you are conveying to the candidate. Candidates are usually more relaxed with a peer than a manager.

Ask the same types of questions to all candidates. This will make it easier for you to evaluate several candidates if you've asked each one of them the same questions; their answers will be simple to compare.

Ask tough questions. Ask "open-ended" questions. Then Listen!

In most interviews, don't reach your decision to make a job offer until you have completed the conversation and have had time to think about it; you want to have collected all relevant information and verified it before you commit to a show of serious interest.

In a few cases when you know you have a winner, you will want to sell hard at the end of the discussion. But, don't commit to an offer or compensation package until you have obtained references and any approvals you may or may not need.

Obtain a completed and signed application from the candidate. You need the signed form in order to have permission to conduct employment references.

Always schedule a second interview. The second interview is a powerful tool in your recruiting process because it tells a candidate that you have a strong interest in hiring him/her. It also shows you that the candidate is also interested in pursuing you and your company. If applicable, you may want to have a senior manager interview the candidate.

You gain support for the hiring decision by having senior management assistance. They help you sell the company as well as give you an additional read on the candidate.

It's extremely important to put together a "Recruitment Package" with information about your company and your branch or area. If you are looking to build a great team, you should always be ready to hand out information on the spot. This gives the candidate an opportunity to take the information home for evaluation. It also keeps you connected with them. So take some time to put together a great package that sells you and your company. Give the candidate compelling reasons why they should join you!

☑ **Checklist**
Select candidate for interview
Outline specific information you wish to get from this candidate; determine what you want to know that he/she hasn't told you yet
Make notes after the interview of facts the candidate has given you about background, experience, etc.
Make sure candidate is interviewed by other staff members
Arrange second interviews with Senior Management if applicable

CHAPTER VI:
The Interview Questions

LEGAL IMPLICATIONS OF INTERVIEW QUESTIONS

The "Legal Questions" which you may ask are:

1) Please provide me with proof of U.S. citizenship.
2) Do you speak a foreign language? Are you fluent?
3) What person can we contact in case of an emergency?
4) Have you ever worked or gone to school under another name?
5) What work-related organizations do you belong to?

The "Illegal Questions" which you may NOT ask are:

1) Where were you born? Where were your parents born?
2) Are you a naturalized citizen? Do you intend to become a citizen?
3) Are you single or married?
4) How old are you? What is your birth date?
5) Are you over 21 years old?
6) What is your religious preference?
7) What "holidays" do you observe?
8) Please supply a recent photograph with your application.
9) How did you learn to speak Spanish/French/etc.?
10) What clubs, societies or lodges do you belong to?
11) How long do you intend to work? (e.g. to expectant mother)
12) How do you plan to provide child care?
13) Do you have any physical or mental handicaps or disabilities?

14) Would your spouse object to your traveling as part of the job?
15) Tell me about your spouse.
16) Do you plan to have children?
17) Do you own your own home?
18) What type of military discharge did you receive?
19) Have you ever been arrested?
20) Please give me names and addresses of your relatives?
21) Tell me your opinion on (religion, politics, racial) issues; e.g., women's lib, elections.
22) Please list the names and ages of minor children or dependents.
23) What is your height and weight?
24) Are you homosexual?
25) Please list your eye color, hair color, and complexion.
26) Have you ever served in a non-U.S. military service?
27) Are you the head of your household?
28) Have you had any prior workers compensation or major health insurance claims?
29) Have you ever been treated for alcoholism or drug use?
30) Do you take any prescription medicine?
31) What is your maiden name, Mrs. Smith?

SAMPLE INTERVIEW QUESTIONS

Job Knowledge

- Describe for me the type/kind of work you do now.
- Where did you develop the skills and gain the knowledge to successfully perform your job?
- What is the most challenging aspect of your current position?
- Tell me about an area where your job knowledge is not as strong as you would like it to be and how you plan to improve your knowledge in this area.
- In what area would your job knowledge qualify you as an expert, and why?
- What do you believe are the most important skills required in this job?
- Think about a problem which you faced in your current job. How did you resolve it?

Customer Relations

- Tell me about a time when a customer really made you angry.
- What experience have you had with a miscommunication with a customer or a fellow employee, and how did you handle it?
- Share with me an occasion when you really went to bat for a customer. What did you do to satisfy the customer's concern, and how did you go about it?
- What do you consider to be the key components of good customer relations, and how did you go about developing these skills and abilities?

Quality of Work

- What aspect of your work quality makes you proud, and why?
- Describe a time when a work assignment didn't meet your supervisor's expectations and what you did to correct the situation.
- How would you define a quality product in your work?
- Tell me about a time when you exerted extra effort to produce a quality product. What did you have to do, and why did you do it?
- Describe a time when you made a mistake that illustrates your need for improvement.
- When you had to do a job that was particularly uninteresting, how did you deal with it?

Motivation/Incentive

- Describe for me what you did at work yesterday.
- Tell me what motivates you in a job.
- If you had the opportunity to write your own job description, how would it read?
- What is an example of a time when a supervisor placed unreasonable expectations on you and how did you respond?
- Tell me about a time when you had to go above and beyond the call of duty in order to complete a job.
- Describe a situation in your last job where you could structure your own work schedule. What did you do?

Team Work

- You've heard the expression "being able to roll with the punches." Describe a time when you had to do that with a difficult person.
- Describe for me two different people with whom you work and how you handle them.
- What attributes make others particularly easy people with whom to work?
- Tell me about a team you have been on which was particularly effective.
- What role do you play on your current work team?
- Tell me about a team experience which was frustrating to you.

Adaptability

- Describe the type of responsibilities you have been asked to assume in the past.
- Give me an example of a time when you had to modify or change your priorities at work.
- Tell me what changes you have been asked to make in the last three months in your work methods or procedures.
- Describe the major obstacles that you had to overcome in your last job and how you handled them.

Reliability

- Tell me about a time when you were not able to follow through on a promise which you made about completing a work assignment.
- Describe a time when a teammate failed to meet a commitment to the work group and the effect this had on the team.
- Describe the time pressures on your job and tell me what you have done to ease those pressures.
- Tell me about an assignment which you had to undertake without much direction from your manager.
- How do you address the factors which place limits on your ability to exercise initiative?

- Tell me about a time when you had to step out of your normal role to see an assignment to completion.

Ethics

- How do you feel about ethics?
- What are your thoughts on "proprietary lending?"
- Describe a time when you felt that you pushed ethical boundaries?
- What are your thoughts on loan fraud?

NOTE: All of these questions are phrased as "open-ended" questions. The candidate must respond with a full answer, and cannot respond simply "yes" or "no."

CHAPTER VII: Referencing for Confirmation

OVERVIEW

You'll want to conduct thorough references on the candidate you wish to hire for several reasons:

- First, you want to confirm that the information he/she has given you is correct. Even if you have known the candidate from a prior working relationship, you should reconfirm what the candidate has been doing since you last worked together.
- Second, you'll want to reconfirm your own evaluation of the candidate by seeking outside opinions, particularly from people who have worked with the candidate as a colleague, boss or customer.

Part of your task in referencing candidates is to uncover any weaknesses or deficiencies. In addition, you want to be sure that you will be able to manage these things if you hire the candidate. What you don't know can hurt you! You are way ahead if you hire a new sales person knowing the good, as well as the "not so good." For example, if a great producer has weak telephone presentation but terrific face-to-face selling skills, you'll know to insist that he/she gets out of the office to call on Realtors or builders. Please don't misunderstand this. This is not micro managing. It's being smart about helping others create the highest and best use for achieving outstanding performance. This benefits all parties.

Very often, you will interview and want to hire someone you know, or someone who is referred to you by someone you know well. You will be tempted to omit the referencing step because you are dealing with a known commodity. When that temptation hits you, ask yourself if every mortgage company will underwrite every loan the same way. The answer is obviously no. The reason you conduct references is that you need to "underwrite" every candidate you are considering. People you've known for a long time can change. The mortgage business changes rapidly and dramatically; someone you knew two years ago to be successful might not be able to make it in today's environment. Your best support for your hiring decision is the unbiased corroboration from other people who know the candidate from other business experiences.

Check it out! Check it out! Check it out!
What you don't know can hurt you!

ACTIONS TO TAKE

- Identify reference sources from two or more of the following categories of people who know the candidate
- Get W-2s to confirm income
- Colleague, either Loan Originator, Processor, or Underwriter
- Realtor/Builder
- Borrower
- Previous Boss or Supervisor
- Broker
- Agency contact
- Personal friend

Obtain a list of references from the candidate, but always tell him/her that you may contact additional people not on the list. Obviously, the candidate will give you names of people who will say positive things about him or her. You'll want to confirm those traits from other unbiased sources as well.

Be sure the candidate knows you plan to check references and be sure you have a signed application from the candidate giving you permission to check references. If he/she asks for you to be discreet and not to jeopardize current employment, you should do so. You can speak to prior employers now, and contact the current employer after the candidate has accepted the job in order to verify your decision. Problems are much easier to solve when caught early. Have you ever heard about the "Godzilla Principle?" This principle is based on the original Godzilla movie. They found a small lizard looking thing. They didn't do anything about it. Next thing they knew, this lizard was trampling down Tokyo! Get Godzilla while he's small, otherwise you won't be able to get him at all!

Where possible, speak to the people with whom the candidate has worked with; avoid the personnel office since they will only be able to tell you dates of employment, title and eligibility for re-hire.

Prepare a script of questions you want to ask each reference about the candidate. The questions you ask a former supervisor may relate to technical knowledge, administrative skills or delegation skills to support staff. By contrast, you want to ask a customer reference about service levels, responsiveness and follow-through.

Tailor your questions to the issues you have about a candidate. Perhaps this candidate seemed to be quiet or a bit shy. You might ask a customer reference about the candidate's ability to initiate contact and be aggressive in solving problems; or, you could ask a former boss or colleague about sales styles and ability to close a sale.

Think about the traits you observed in the interview process that you liked, or did not like; and ask the reference to confirm that trait. Sometimes, an individual will put on "interview manners" and show you one type of behavior during the interview process; but he/she behaves very differently in "real life." You might ask a former boss to describe how the candidate handled a particular transaction (e.g. a denied loan, an upset Realtor, builder or borrower, abrupt market changes) and see if that description matches your impression of the candidate.

Remember that there are always legal issues to observe when obtaining a reference (see Chapters VI and XI).

Sometimes, the person you are questioning about a candidate will be evasive or not give you a direct answer. This may be an indication to you have a problem, and you will have to decide if the issue being avoided is serious or not. As in the interview discussion, your most important task is to evaluate the information you are being given. Listen carefully to what a reference says, what is not said, or how it is said.

Document every reference call you make, including the ones who don't call you back. Be sure to note the date and time of the call, the person to whom you spoke, his/her relationship with the candidate, how long he/she knew the candidate, and the responses to your scripted questions. Keep the reference notes with your candidate file.

Candidate Name:	
Reference Name:	Date Called:
Position:	Phone #:
Company:	
Address:	
Relationship to Candidate:	
# Years Known Candidate:	
Comments:	

☑ Checklist
Identify at least three references, including at least one not given to you by the candidate
Prepare script for each reference you call before you make the call
Make notes of each reference call

CHAPTER VIII:

Extending and Negotiating the Job Offer

Why Should They Work For You? How Are You Different?

OVERVIEW

You have gone through all of the recruiting steps; you have identified a candidate you want to hire; you have obtained fantastic references; you are ready to make a job offer. This is the easy part, right? Well, maybe or maybe not.

Just like in sales, you must sell your company and what you have to offer to cause the candidate to want to work for you. What makes you differenct from other companies out here? How do you support your loan officers growth and productivity? What's it like to work for you? Just like a sales person must have a strong positioning statement, so should you. What do you have to offer? What is your company's mission and culture? Make sure they know all of the upside to working at your company.

At this point, you need to be sure that not only have you gotten all the information you need to make a good decision, but that your candidate has had all of his/her questions answered as well. Too often, our enthusiasm for the process may ignore the candidate's need for information, encouragement or support to make a job change. All along the process, you should ask the candidate if he/she has any questions; However, questions may arise as a result of learning more about you and your company.

Almost universally, the toughest types of questions at this point revolve around money. Before you make a job offer, you should know clearly and specifically what expectations the candidate has about the compensation plan. Do not make any promises or guarantees about earnings, signing bonuses, pipeline buyouts, and/or commission splits before you have approval for the offer. But, you should be able to get the candidate to describe his/her current compensation plan and how he/she wants to improve it. When you ask about expectations, always let the candidate tell you what's important to him/her, because it is likely to be different for each person you interview.

Be sure you are familiar with the current, approved compensation plans for your company. In addition to being familiar with your company's compensation plan for new hires; you should also be familiar with what the competition's compensation packages are so that you know what you're up against. The more you know about the competition and the candidate's expectation, the better you'll be able to choose a structure that will work for him/her, and you'll offer only as much as you need to get an acceptance. This puts you in a stronger position and increases the odds of getting the candidates acceptance.

"Always negotiate from a position of power"

ACTIONS TO TAKE

Once you've completed the references, tell the candidate that you want to extend a job offer. Ask him/her if there are any key issues that should be addressed on the offer that you have not yet discussed. These could include start date, equipment (computers, pagers, cellular phones), non-compete agreements, or the like, as well as compensation plan issues. Be honest with the candidate and let them know how long it will take for you to obtain the proper approvals.

Ask specifically if the candidate has signed any agreement with his/her current company that might limit the candidate's actions as our employee. Limitations might include solicitation of current customers, hiring of employees, or similar actions. If the candidate has signed any type of document, ask for a copy and have it reviewed by senior management or the Legal Department if applicable.

You are now ready to communicate the job offer in a face-to-face meeting with the candidate. It is to your advantage to gauge reaction if you are face-to-face. You should be delivering good news, and you will want to close the deal on the spot, if possible. If any part of the offer is not what the candidate wanted, explain why you were not able to comply with his/her request, but offer an alternative solution to an unfulfilled request if possible. You are the best able to gauge the candidate's reaction to the job offer if you extend it in person.

Remember that some people have a hard time making a job change. Even top sales people get comfortable where they are, and can be reluctant to move. Be enthusiastic about the new job, and be sure that the candidate knows that you really want him/her to accept the offer and join your team.

Consider a follow-up call from other people in the office, or from the company's owner, and/or senior management. This could help close the deal. Even if the candidate accepts immediately, these types of calls will help welcome your new Loan Originator to the office and start the employment process on a positive note.

If the candidate has any hesitation about accepting the offer, try to determine the reason for the hesitation so you can address it. If he/she wants to "think about it," always give the candidate a specific time in which to respond. Every situation is different. Generally, you should get a response within 48 hours or less. I have found that if it takes longer than 48 hours, the candidate has other offers and you could loose them if you don't stay connected here.

OVERCOMING OBJECTIONS

We all know that overcoming objections is part of life. Especially the life of a mortgage production manager. The first step to overcoming an objection is to:

1. Understand the objection by restating the objection and asking questions.
2. Make sure the objection is true and accurate. You may get an objection that your rates are too high. First of all, find out what makes the candidate believe that your rates are too high. Secondly, is it true that your rates are too high?

If you get through 1 and 2 above, the objections then become easy to deal with. If you do get into an area where you have disagreement with the candidate, you must deal with it as best you can. You will come to a point when that particular issue is one you don't want to focus on.

If it becomes a problem, begin discussing areas that will be beneficial by hiring the candidate. Key in on those areas and benefits that will make you and the candidate a great team. Remember, communication is everything. The following are some objection examples and how to respond:

1. Your compensation plan is too low?

- Compared to what?
- Let's do the arithmetic on your production to review the difference.
- Based on our research, we are more competitive for the higher achievers.
- We have a wide variety of loan products, which open up selling opportunities. (Remember, don't just tell them, show them...educate them!)

2. Your rates are too high?

- Compared to whom?
- We are Loan Originator driven, not price driven. Let me show you what I mean. (Give examples here on how much you support your loan originators.)
- We have a wide variety of loan products.
- We are a well-balanced company; it doesn't make sense to fund loans at a loss.
- We are in this business for the long haul, we hope you are also.

THE TWO BIGGEST REASONS FOR OBJECTIONS ARE:

1. People fear making a change or a wrong decision, and/or…
2. You have not created enough value.

"If you want fewer objections, ask more questions. If you want more business, create more trust. If you have the client's best interest in mind, questions are easy and trust is natural. If questions are easy and trust is natural, the close will happen almost automatically."

"If two people want to do business together, the details won't get in the way. If two people don't want to do business together, the details won't make it happen."

-Tony Alessandra

Get good at managing objections by using the 5 step objection response model:

THE 5 STEP OBJECTION RESPONSE MODEL	
STEP 1:	**Honor the objection as the prospect's right.** "I appreciate and understand your concern about...tell me more about what happened."
STEP 2:	**Ask a Question:** "Tell me what it is about the objection that makes you feel uncomfortable moving forward?"
STEP 3:	**Listen** Shut up!
STEP 4:	**Isolate** "Suppose I could help you to get comfortable with the objection, would we have a basis for a business relationship?"
STEP 5:	**Use a script, answer the objection and ask for the business.** The objection given is rarely the real objection. By discovering the real issues that are preventing them from saying yes, you can take the relationship to the next level.

Use scripts to master the art of managing objections:

PRIOR BAD EXPERIENCE OBJECTIONS:

SCRIPT #1: YOUR COMPANY OR OTHER COMPANY

"The last thing I want is for a previous bad experience to prevent you from enjoying many good experiences in the future. Share with me what happened. (Let prospect expand). My role is to make your relationship with me risk-free. Making me aware of this was the first step. My communicating this concern with my team is the second step. And third, I am totally committed to making sure that as long as you are doing business with me, this will never happen. Here's how…(state your strategy). Based on that, do you feel we have a basis for moving forward in a business relationship?"

✓ Checklist
Determine that all of the candidate's questions have been answered
Develop the job offer; prepare the compensation plan recommendation
Obtain all necessary approvals (If applicable)
Communicate offer to candidate in person
Arrange follow-up calls to encourage candidate to accept offer

CHAPTER IX:
Closing the Process

OVERVIEW

Now that you have successfully recruited your top choice candidate, you need to conclude the process by completing the administrative details. You owe it to your newly hired superstar that all of the paperwork to get him/her started and paid promptly is done—-and done correctly!

You also want to make sure that you close out any other candidates whom you interviewed, as well as thank people in your network who referred candidates to you. A simple "thank you" can go a long way to insure that a referral source continues to send top candidates to you.

Let me emphasize the importance of taking care of people every step of the way. One of the reasons I've been so successful over the years in recruiting is because I treat all people the way I want to be treated and it works! For example: When I receive 10 resumes from new or experienced loan officers, I interview all of them, yet only hire a few. However, I always contact the ones I didn't hire to let them know why and give them some advice, if possible.

Remember, people always appreciate communication. I have done this when hiring processors, underwriters, closers etc, as well. People will remember and appreciate you for being honest and considering their feelings. This has caused tremendous benefit for my company and me. I have had originators that I did not hire, go to work for someone else, become top producers, and eventually ended up working for me because of the way they were treated in the past. Treating people right comes back to you!

It is critical to make sure that the new loan officer has a proper place to work with all of the proper office equipment. It is also critical that you set some time aside on their first day to introduce them to the office personnel, show them around the office, show them how to work all of the office equipment, and make sure that they get comfortable as soon as possible. The quicker they get settled, the quicker the loan production starts rolling in. There is nothing worse than to start with a new company and be lost. Show you really care by taking the time and making the time. Show that you are excited about having them be a part of your team by having their business cards, pagers, cell phone, etc....ready for them when they start. It's also a great idea to have balloon and flowers on their desk when they start. Celebrate as much as possible. How would you feel if your employer did that for you on your first day of work?

Finally, review all of your notes, logs and information in the recruiting file you created for this opening. Complete the applicant log, close your candidate log, retain the resumes and completed applications for future reference, and generally clean out the file.

"Progressively treat others exactly like you want to be treated"

ACTIONS TO TAKE

- Order business cards, nametags, appropriate manuals and desk equipment in time to arrive before the Loan Originator's first day of work.
- As soon as you have an acceptance, commitment, and start date from your candidate, you should notify other candidates whom you interviewed that the job is filled. Be polite, business like, and explain to them why you made the decision you made. It is important here that you be honest and polite. You never know when you'll meet up with this person down the road. I always like to assume that I will need this candidate at some point in the future.
- Call each of the people in your referral network who provided names and explain that you have filled the job. You'll want to let your network know that you appreciate their help, so that you can ask them to help in the future.
- Be sure your new employee knows where to report to work, what time you expect him/her on the first day, and what information he/she needs to bring (e.g., proof of citizenship, social security number, etc.)

- Complete all "New Hire" paperwork according to your company guidelines. Make sure that all paperwork is completed correctly and with no delay.
- Be ready for them! There is nothing worse than starting a new job when the emplyer doesn't seem to be organized.
- Be sure you personally introduce the new salesperson to everyone in the office, and describe each person's duties. Generally, it's a nice gesture to take the new Loan Originator to lunch on his/her first day, preferably with other sales people who can help make him/her feel welcome.
- Clean out the recruiting file for this job opening and be sure all logs are completed appropriately. Retain resumes and applications for future reference.

☑ Checklist
Order business cards, name tags, manuals to be available by start date
Notify other candidates that job is filled
Thank people in network who referred candidates
Complete new hire paperwork. This should be accomplished by start date
Clean out recruiting file; complete logs; retain resumes and completed applications
Confirm start date, time and location with candidate
Introduce new Loan Originator to all staff in branch

CHAPTER X:
Retaining Your Best People

It's pretty simple to say, but can be very difficult to do. The key to retaining your best people long term is to build solid relationships and friendships with them. We've all heard of "Relationship Selling." Relationship Selling is important if we want to keep life-long customers. This is a powerful way to get and retain customers over long periods of time. So, how can we apply increased relationships in other areas? How about "Relationship Managing?" The Wall Sreet Journal did a survey of the top CEOs in the United States. They found that 70 percent of the decisions that CEOs make are based on their relationships with friends. Their business decisions are based on input from their friends because of the relationship they have together. We tend to seek advice from several sources, a business associate, colleague, partner, customers, boss, and/or peers. But in general, friends have a huge impact on what decisions we make. We tend to become like the people we hang around with. We have all heard the old axiom, "It's not what you know, and it's whom you know." I believe that in order to survive in today's competitive environment, it is both – it's what you know and whom you know.

How many of you have ever had a loan processor quit because he or she was offered more money from another company? How many have ever had a loan originator quit for the same reason? My next question is; "What must we do to keep this from happening or at least minimize the damages?" In addition, "Can we retain top producing people in mortgage origination long term?" The business has become more splintered with the onset of net branches, franchising, mega lenders, small to mid size broker shops, etc. It may be more difficult today, but it can be done and is being done consistently. The secret to building life-long or career-long loyalties is caring about the person and their personal goals, paying them extremely well, and building solid relationships with them.

Relationship management is increasingly important in today's mortgage origination environment. Look at relationship management as insurance. If you invest some extra time building relationships with your team, the chance of you seeing them recruited away decreases. You'll never be able to keep 100 percent of your top people all the time. We're merely seeking some strategies and distinctions that will increase our effectiveness and decrease our turnover. This is an essential distinction that must be taken seriously to add some security to your business.

When I hear managers talk about loan originators, it is usually in the negative. I hear managers say; "Those loan officers only care about themselves. Those loan officers will leave you for the slightest thing. Every loan officer is greedy. They will leave you for more money every time. Loan officers are all high ego sales people who only care about themselves." Do some of these comments sound familiar? All of these statements have been true at one time or another, but it is definitely not like this all the time. In fact, many managers tend to contribute to the problem of the "us and them" syndrome. Let's stop all this madness. Let me give you some key concepts on how we can improve our relationships and reputations with loan originators.

First, we must understand that all employees (not just loan officers) listen to radio station WII-FM (What's in it for me?") In fact, all human beings listen to this radio station most of the time. By realizing this simple fact, we can adjust the way we think about this issue. If we understand that all people are this way to a certain degree, it is easier to understand that one particular loan officer who is on our mind. Why shouldn't we ask our loan officers, "What's in it for you?" A good recruiter of loan officers will always ask this. But as soon as we hire them, we find ourselves talking negative about them at our first manager's meeting.

Think about it – if our ongoing goal is to help them "be all they can be," we can't lose if we seek to understand them first. In Steven Covey's book, "Seven Habits of Highly Successful People," this is one of the habits. Seek first to understand, then to be understood. Sure, a few bad apples might stab you in the back, but if you treat them right, these incidences become rare. The bottom line is that most people will want to help you if they feel you really care. So let's start by refraining from saying negative things about loan officers and how they tend to be high-maintenance individuals who only care about themselves. Let's practice the art and science of being positive more often. It doesn't matter how smart a manager is. If you can't say something nice about your own people, don't say anything at all. I know you've heard that before...maybe from your mother? Growing up, my mother has told me that about one hundred times. Can you tell I have siblings?

Let's look at WII-FM as a positive and see how far we get. Zig Ziglar said it best, "If you help enough other people get what they want, then you'll get what you want." Besides listening to WII-FM, it is also important to motivate your loan officers. Your ability to motivate other people will depend on how you answer these two questions. Can you motivate others? What environment are you creating? Let me give you the answers and we'll review this concept.

Can you motivate other people? The correct answer is no! You can't motivate others because they have to motivate themselves. You can motivate them short-term, but it's not going to last until they learn to motivate themselves. Have you ever been to a motivational seminar? Were you motivated and how long did the motivation last? Even if you went to see Zig Ziglar, one of the greatest motivational speakers of all time, your motivation doesn't usually last unless you yourself make it last. It doesn't last because someone else (other than you) is doing the motivating. You must seek out and learn what motivates you personally. This is the only way to stay motivated over long periods of time. It's also the only way we can help others stay motivated. If you can't motivate yourself, how are you going to motivate others in your workplace? We don't have the ability to motivate other people long-term, however, we can learn what motivates them, and then support that. This is the key. This is a way that you can assist people in motivating themselves. Another reason for the difficulty in motivating others is that everyone is different. What motivates you may not motivate me at all. What motivates me may not motivate someone else. The most important thing in keeping good people at any position is to find out what motivates them and support whatever it is. For example, I once had a loan officer who wanted to get into management. This person was not ready for management, yet I supported him by sending him to good management seminars when they came along. I would also buy him a management book or two. This showed him that I cared about him and his goals. I gained by achieving long-term loyalty and production from this individual before he went on into management. I firmly believe that he would have left me a lot sooner if I didn't support his goals. I know this because he told me.

The second question is, "What environment are you creating?" For several years, I consulted for several mortgage banking and mortgage brokerage firms. Every time I would walk into a mortgage office, I could tell how successful it was. If they have cheap furniture, I'd look around and say, "Wow, you must be profitable." But seriously, the successful branches have energy and life and it's evident when you walk in. The branches that are less successful don't have as much energy and life. When people go to work every day, they go to "an environment." Some environments are negative and some are positive. What environment do you walk into everyday? What can you do to improve your work environment? It all starts with the manager. As you go, so goes your team. As the manager goes, so goes the team. As the leader goes, so goes the team. Do you have energy? Do you walk and talk with purpose? Do you support your personal message with the way the office is decorated and furnished? Do you have positive affirmations posted around the office? Is your personal drive and focus to help you, or to help your loan officers, or both? These are empowering questions that you should ask and answer. Then you can find ways to improve on the answer to every question. Your office should reflect your company culture and mission for being in business. Don't keep this a secret. People want to be a part of something! Let that be you and your organization.

Another critical aspect of improving your relationships with your people is to praise and appreciate them. Ken Blanchard, author of The One-Minute Manager, found that appreciation is the number one tool any manager could use for effectiveness. In fact, in all the surveys that I've read, the number one reason as to why people work is always "appreciation and contribution." Both of these come before money. As they say, if you're only working for a paycheck...that is all you'll ever get. All people want and need appreciation. Thank them for doing a good job, even though it's just their job. In other words, thank them for doing their job, but reward them for going above and beyond the call of duty.

Dr. Steven Covey says that our relationships with others are like a bank account. If you make deposits in your bank account, you can make a withdrawal occasionally. Like relationships, if you make positive emotional deposits (like praise) in other people, you can afford an occasional withdrawal. But if you never make positive deposits, you bankrupt the account or the relationship. In marriage, we call that divorce. Moreover, we do not want to go there if we can help it, and we can!

When you praise people on your mortgage origination team for doing a good job, follow these guidelines:

- **1. Tell them what they did right and be specific**. For example: "Mike, I want to thank you for doing such a great job on the Smith loan. I know that loan was a tough loan and not many loan officers would have been able to pull it off. Great job!
- **2. Tell them how you feel about it. For example:** Mike, it makes me feel good to know that I can count on you to do a great job, even on the difficult loans such as the Smith loan. I really do appreciate working with you Mike.
- **3. Encourage more of the same and be sincere**. For example: "I wish I could clone you Mike, keep up the great job!

If you tie these three steps together when you praise someone, you will be making a large, positive, emotional deposit for your own future success. In addition, they will feel great about themselves, which leads to improved performance. Turnover will go down and employee contentment will go up.

Finally, take the time to be with your loan officers. Look at them as people first, loan officers second. Always remember that people work for people first, causes second. If Hitler didn't lead people into evil, they would have never gone there. People do follow causes, however there is always a driving force (some person) behind the cause. Be a person of positive influence for your team and the people you work with by caring about them and investing some time with them. Especially your key people! Your key people will help you expand your relationships and leadership to others in the organization.

One idea is to have them over for dinner. Do activities outside the workplace with them. Be proactive in building a solid relationship with your people. Please keep balanced in what I'm saying here. I'm not saying that you should stay up all night and close the local bars down with your team every night. In fact, you need to be smart about your conduct with the people you work with. Treat people with dignity and respect and don't be afraid to do things that are "appropriate" outside the workplace. It's okay to be friends with the people you work with. Use common sense.

All friendships and relationships require an investment of time. A survey recently conducted at a local middle school. The speaker asked the students, "How many of you have friends?" Ninety-five percent of the students raised their hands. Then he asked, "How many of you have good friends?" Only 75 percent of the students raised their hands. Then he asked, "How many of you have best friends?" Only 25 percent of the students raised their hands. Then he asked, "Is there anyone better than a best friend?" Three girls in the back raised their hands and responded, "yes there is!" The girls said that a "true" friend is better than a best friend because no matter what secrets you tell a "true" friend, they will not repeat it to anyone else. The speaker asked, "How long does it take to build a "true" friendship with someone?" The three girls responded by saying that they were "true" friends with each other and spend about six hours per day together. The point is that an investment of time is necessary for improving your relationships with your loan officers and staff.

One of the best investments you can make in your mortgage future is to take the time and make the time with helping your own team succeed. In measuring how much time you should spend with the people on your team depends on how successful they are or on how much desire they have. I have always invested a lot of time in my top performers as well as those people who had a burning desire to succeed. Use common sense here. You don't want to spend too much time with high maintenance/low producing people. Focusing on supporting your people because they are your internal customers. If you serve your internal customers (employees, co-workers, your team) better, they will serve the external customers (borrowers, Realtors, builders, financial planners) better. If the external customers receive better service, production and profits increase! It is a wonderful thing to be able to help someone with his or her career and make a friend in the process.

I'm not giving you a "Pollyanna" approach to your business and I am not saying you should go out and try to be best friends with all of your employees. What I am saying is to go out and deliberately find ways to improve the relationship you have with the people you work with. In addition to being good for your health, good relationships can have a profound effect on your bottom line.

In summary, remember to manage effectively by finding ways to improve your relationships with your employees, always speak positively when referring to your loan officers and others, give them effective praise often, and make the time to get to know your people better. If you will help them get what they want, you'll get what you want.

☑ Checklist
Do I gossip about my own people?
Am I talking positive or negative to others about my people?
Am I praising effectively? Be specific, tell them how you feel, and encourage more of the same positive behaviors/actions.
Have I asked each of my people what motivates them?
Action steps to support their own goals (not mine or the company')
What action steps have I taken to get to know them better?

CHAPTER XI: What You Should Know About Employment Law

Of the top three resources we have in the workplace today, financial resources, physical resources, and human resources, which one of these resources takes the most time and money to manage. You'd be correct if you answer human resources. Dealing with people is the biggest challenge we have. In this chapter, I'm going to give you some legal guidelines for you to follow in the areas of hiring as well as managing people in the workplace.

It's important for you to know what your local state laws are so that you can determine specific actions to take in all situations. It's also critical to seek the advice of legal counsel as every situation is different and laws are constantly changing. Many states are "At Will" states. At will means that both the employer and the employee are "At Will" when it comes to voluntary or involuntary termination of employment. That means that an employee can quit or be fired without notice or cause. In reality, "at will" is difficult to enforce because of all the discrimination laws in place. In other words, you could fire an employee for no reason and they could claim that you did it because of some form of discrimination. The at will law gets sideswiped all the time by Title VII discrimination laws.

The Americans with Disabilities Act (ADA) of 1990 and the Civil Rights Act of 1991 have an underlying goal of providing fair, impartial, and rationally based job opportunities to all people. Failure to follow this precept in hiring can be very costly to the organization.

Most people who do interviewing are aware that the Civil Rights Act of 1964 has made it illegal to discriminate against a job applicant on the basis of race, age, religion, sex, or national origin. Persons in each of these groups fall into a "protected class." The Americans with Disabilities Act of 1990 extends similar protection to persons with disabilities. By "protected," the law means that special care and consideration must be given to applicants in each of these categories. The majority of all workers in America now fall into at least one of these protected classes.

THE LEGAL BASIS

The major piece of legislation that affects employment is the Civil Rights Act of 1964. The foundation of anti-discrimination hiring legislation if found in Title 7 of that Act:

> "It shall be an unlawful employment practice for an employer-(1) to fail or refuse to hire or to discharge any individual, or otherwise to discriminate against an individual with respect to his compensation, terms, conditions, or privileges of employment because of such individual's race, color, religion, sex, or national origin, or (2) to limit, segregate, classify his employees in any way which would deprive or tend to deprive any individual of employment opportunities or other wise adversely affect his status as an employee, because of such an individual's race, color, religion, sex or national origin."

In the almost three decades that have ensued since the Civil Rights Act of 1964, many additional pieces of legislation, a variety of court decisions, and presidential executive orders have been put in place to ensure that workers in the United States receive fair and equal opportunity.

The Americans with Disabilities Act of 1990 (ADA) enacted on July 26, 1990, was designed to eliminate discrimination against individuals with all forms of disabilities. Congress defined a person with disabilities as one who has a "mental or physical impairment that substantially limits at least one major life activity, who has a record of an impairment, or who is regarded as having an impairment." The definition of impairment and disability is extremely broad. The ADA is enforced by the federal Equal Employment Opportunity Commission (EEOC) and state Equal Employment Opportunity (EEO) agencies.

The intention of the ADA is to ensure fairness, not to compel an employer to hire individuals who are incapable of performing the job. Anyone with the qualifications and ability to perform the essential functions of a job must be given equal consideration. DO not ask an applicant any questions about his/her health or the nature or extent of any disability.

Asking applicants any type of question about their personal background, living situation, number of children at home, other sources of income, plans for the future, etc., are all viewed as inappropriate. In organizations that do operate on other than the traditional nine-to-five, Monday-through-Friday schedule, a legitimate concern for the employer is whether people are available for shift work, overtime, out-of-town travel, and a variety of other schedules.

Personal questioning is never appropriate in a job interview. It has been illegal to ask people certain questions about their personal lives for the past two decades. This sort of information is not likely to be useful in predicting success in the job. Divorces, stepfamilies, relocation spouses, marriages, and pregnancies will all continue to occur in the future. These matters are of no relevance to the employment interview.

If the job requires overtime, travel or weekend work, then the employer has a right to know whether or not the candidate can meet this job requirement. Use closed-end questions to determine whether a person is available for short-notice overtime, travel, or weekend work. Ask the questions of all people who are interviewed for the position. State the job requirement clearly, consistently, and accurately and ask if the requirement poses any difficulty for the candidate. The person can give a "yes" or "no" answer. The candidates should be advised of the consequences of their failure to meet these particular job requirements in the future. Discuss job requirements and the disruption an individual would cause by failing to meet the job requirement.

THE IDEAL SELECTION PROCESS

Ideally, every selection procedure should have several standard elements:

Job Analysis. The first component of such a system would be that of a professional job analysis. Reliable sources of expertise are used to define the requirements for successfully completing the job.

Good Selection Criteria. The second area is the use of appropriate selection criteria. The criteria need to reflect the actual job requirements (based on the job analysis) and should be stated in observable, measurable, behavioral terms.

Terminology such as "hard charging," "competitive," "team player," or " nice personality" should be avoided. Selection criteria should be defined as competencies that an individual possesses or is likely to possess within a reasonable period of time after being employed.

Standard Procedure. The third area of concern is equivalent or standard treatment. All applicants for a job should be treated in similar or equivalent ways. If a forty-five minute screening interview is routinely conducted at the beginning of a job selection process, give all candidates the opportunity to be interviewed for forty-five minutes. Even a person who is clearly unqualified for the job, must be given the full allotment of time—unless they ask to be excused. If questions from three areas of competency are typically asked, ask each candidate the same number of questions even though they may be worded slightly differently.

Documentation. You should keep an accurate and objective set of notes from the interview. These notes should be factual, professional, include direct quotes, and should avoid any reference to prohibited or sensitive topics or to impressions formed during the interview.

The responsibility of an interviewer requires the use of good common sense. Use an interviewing system that has a valid and reliable history of predicting success.

As discussed earlier, the top three resources we have in the workplace today, financial resources, physical resources, and human resources. Human resources takes the most time and money to manage. I'm going to give you five steps to keep from being sued.

I want to keep this simple because I'm not an attorney, nor do I claim to be. In fact, I can't guarantee you won't be sued in the future. However, by practicing these five steps, it dramatically reduces the risk of being sued in addition to dramatically increasing the chances of you winning if you are sued.

- **STEP #1: LISTEN TO YOUR PEOPLE!** Most of the attorney's, judges and courts today agree that practicing good listening skills is the best insurance you have to keep from being sued. Think about it, most lawsuits start with someone who is disgruntled. Being disgruntled usually starts with someone who feels like they weren't listened to. If a human being gets the impression or perception that you or your organization does not care, a problem is born. The problem is that many of these problems develop into lawsuits. Listen to your people! When people feel listened to, they are less apt to sue.

STEP #2: BE CONSISTENT! Consistency is key. Treat all employees and co-workers the same when it comes to issues such as company policies, job descriptions, incentives, discipline, and general systems within the workplace. Please don't misunderstand me here. When it comes to motivation, praise, and coaching, we're all taught to treat people different. This is true because different things motivate people. Please keep these two things separate.

For example, you MUST be consistent in the manner in which you provide incentives for your loan officers, receptionists, processors, underwriters and the like. It's a dangerous practice to offer one underwriter a day off if a certain number of loans get underwritten within a certain time period and not offer this same reward to other underwriters within the organization. This is a form of discrimination that you will want to stay away from.

STEP #3: DOCUMENT, DOCUMENT, DOCUMENT. If something is not documented and you have a problem surface, then it's the "he said-she said" game and many times judges and juries don't know whom to believe. If it's documented, it becomes very difficult to dispute by the other party.

Documenting is a discipline that must not be overlooked. It goes a long way in keeping you and your organization out of trouble.

STEP #4: HAVE A LEGITIMATE BUSINESS REASON FOR EVERY DECISION YOU MAKE. Evaluate the purpose for every decision that you make on the job. Especially if you're disciplining or terminating someone. If you have a solid business reason for your actions, the courts are much more understanding about why you did what you did.

- **STEP #5: KEEP YOUR HUMAN RESOURCE DEPARTMENT INVOLVED.** If you have an HR department, keep them involved. If you don't have an HR department, there are several companies that provide human resource services for a fee. Hire them if you have any concern over any issue that comes up. Human Resource professionals are experts at doing things right when it comes to legalities. Keep them in the loop!

A SUCCESS STORY

A woman got a job as an administrative assistant. She and her boss got along great from the first time they met. They immediately began teasing, joking, and bantering with each other. But after a while, she felt he had crossed the line.

She filed a complaint of sexual harassment with the personnel department. They investigated by talking to the boss and to the other workers in the area. They determined sexual harassment had not occurred, because she had welcomed the sexual teasing.

She didn't agree with the decision, so she filed a lawsuit against him in federal court. She continued working for him. But after a while, she felt uncomfortable working for someone she was suing. SO she went to a doctor. He put her out on stress disability leave. After two years, the case was still going on, and her doctor cleared her to return to work.

She went back and was given another administrative assistant job, at the same grade level, reporting to the same boss. After two weeks she quit and filed another lawsuit claiming retaliation. She said the tasks she was given to do were not as good as before. He was denied management-training classes. And she claimed her boss wouldn't talk to her about anything except work.

The sexual harassment and retaliation cases were consolidated for trial. At trial, the judge found she had not been sexually harassed. But that did not dispose of her retaliation claim. Even if she was not harassed, she still might have been retaliated against.

On the retaliation claim, the judge found that the jobs she was given were not as good as the jobs she'd been given before. She was denied management training. And he found that the manager wouldn't talk to her socially.

But the manager and the company won the lawsuit. And they won it because they followed the five key steps.

- **1. He listened.** In this case, his listening did not stop the lawsuit. But he did listen and follow proper procedure.
- **2. He was consistent.** The jobs he gave her to do were the same type of jobs he gave other administrative assistants.
- **3. He documented everything:** the jobs he gave her, the jobs he gave other assistants, and why he denied her management training.
- **4. He had a legitimate business reason for not giving her management training** – she wasn't a manager and she wasn't on a management track. And he had a legitimate business reason for not talking with her socially, since he was scared to death he would get sued again.
- **5. He called an expert.** He had human resource department involved every step of the way, for an independent and professional perspective on his decisions.

Keep your chances of being sued low and your chances of winning high by following the above five steps. More important, if you follow these five key steps, you will treat employees fairly. Fairness is the spirit of employment law.

CHAPTER XII: Job Descriptions

Job Title: Loan Officer
Department: Loan Production
Reports to: Branch/Area Manager

I. Job Summary:

Through professional persistence, solicit and originate investment quality loans that are acceptable to the companies chosen investors and agencies. To be knowledgeable and articulate regarding all aspects of the loan products offered such as FHA/VA, FHLMC, FNMA, JUMBO and all other Area, City, State, County and National loan programs that the company offers. Develop and maintain a strong client referral base by selling the firm's loan products and services to meet the needs of it's client base such as Realtors, builders, home buyers, CPA's, financial planners, and others.

II. Duties & Responsibilities

- To establish, develop and maintain client referral relationships with Realtors, builders, Developers, CPA's, financial planners and make sales calls on potential or existing Customers in order to develop new business and/or retain existing business.
- To keep informed of trends, changes and developments in the local real estate market.
- To keep up with what competitors are doing. To keep up-to-date with changing rules, regulations and guidelines from FNMA, FHLMC, FHA, and VA in addition to other investors and agencies.

- To keep informed of all origination, processing, appraisal, underwriting and closing requirements for both company and investor guidelines pertaining to both government insured and privately insured mortgages.
- Negotiate price, terms and conditions with mortgagors.
- Responsible for the overall customer interaction and interface with all parties involved on each individual loan that is originated from application to closing including, but not limited to: counseling and pre-qualifying potential home buyers; taking complete and accurate applications; obtaining all necessary support documents along with the appropriate fees and lock-in information; overseeing the loan process by monitoring loan status and ensuring conformity with terms; assisting in collecting additional documents and promptly communication loan status to all interested parties; and obtaining loan documentation after closing as directed by corporate or senior management.
- Maintain a professional image and standards consistent with company policies and procedures.

III. Job Dimensions:

Internal Relations: Processors, closer, supervisors, managers, and underwriters.

External Relations: Realtors and brokers, builders, developers, applicants, appraisers title companies, CPAs, financial planners, pest control companies, home inspection companies, Boards and Associations.

Other: This is a commissioned position for which compensation is based on performance and closed loan volume. Responsible for origination loan volume to cover, at a minimum, their draw, business expenses, and benefit coverage expenses. In the event production falls below the minimum employment expenses, probation or termination may result.

IV. Job Specification/Requirements

Minimum 1 to 2 years of loan originator experience or strong sales experience with demonstrated potential to transfer skills to mortgage origination.

Proven ability to read, write, and communicate at a level consistent with the requirements of this position and to generate independent leads for new business.

Working knowledge of standard loan products in the industry and strong familiarity with underwriting guidelines.

Must be able to work flexible hours and be willing to do some travel. Must possess a valid driver's license in the appropriate state(s).

Basic Skill Sets Required: Math Skills, Communication Skills, Interpersonal Relationship Skills, Sales Skills, Social Skills and Leadership Skills. This job requires the individual to have a balanced combination of "People/Social Skills," and at the same time be "Detail Oriented" with strong follow-up skills.

Job Title: Managing Loan Officer
Department: Loan Production
Reports to: Branch/Area Manager or Senior Management

I. Job Summary:

Through professional persistence, solicit and originate investment quality loans that are acceptable to the company's chosen investors and agencies. To be knowledgeable and articulate regarding all aspects of the loan products offered such as FHA/VA, FHLMC, FNMA, JUMBO and all other Area, City, State, County and National loan programs that the company offers. Develop and maintain strong client referral base by selling the firm's loan products and services to meet the needs of it's client base such as Realtors, builders, home buyers, CPA's, financial planners, and others.

II. Duties & Responsibilities

- To establish, develop and maintain client referral relationships with Realtors, builders, developers, CPA's, financial planners and make sales calls on potential or existing customers in order to develop new business and/or retain existing business.
- To hire, train, and manage the loan officer staff in accordance with company

and industry standards. This is to include training and mentoring in areas such as product knowledge and sales training.

- To keep informed of trends, changes and developments in the local real estate market. To keep up with what competitors are doing. To keep up-to-date with changing rules, regulations and guidelines from FNMA, FHLMC, FHA, and VA in addition to other investors and agencies.
- To keep informed of all origination, processing, appraisal, underwriting and closing requirements for both company and investor guidelines pertaining to both government insured and privately-insured mortgages.
- Negotiate price, terms and conditions with mortgagors.
- Responsible for the overall customer interaction and interface with all parties involved on each individual loan that is originated from application to closing including, but not limited to: counseling and pre-qualifying potential home buyers; taking complete and accurate applications; obtaining all necessary support documents along with the appropriate fees and lock-in information; overseeing the loan process by monitoring loan status and ensuring conformity with terms; assisting in collecting additional documents and promptly communication loan status to all interested parties; and obtaining loan documentation after closing as directed by corporate or senior management.
- Maintain a professional image and standards consistent with company policies and procedures.

III. Job Dimensions:

Directly Supervises: Loan Officers

Internal Relations: Processors, closer, supervisors, managers, and underwriters.

External Relations: Realtors and brokers, builders, developers, applicants, appraisers title companies, CPAs, financial planners, pest control companies, home inspection companies, Boards and Associations.

Other: This compensation is based on performance for not only individual performance, but also on the performance of the Loan Originators under your guidance. This is based on closed loan volume of high quality mortgage loans, which are salable on the secondary mortgage market. In addition to personal production and Loan Originator production, manager is responsible for overseeing bottom-line and profitability as well.

IV. Job Specification/Requirements

Minimum 1 to 2 years of loan originator experience, strong sales experience and experience of managing and supervising others.

Proven ability to read, write, and communicate at a level consistent with the requirements of this position and to generate independent leads for new business.

Working knowledge of standard loan products in the industry and strong familiarity with underwriting guidelines.

Must be able to work flexible hours and be willing to do some travel. Must possess a valid driver's license in the appropriate state(s).

Basic Skill Sets Required: Math Skills, Communication Skills, Interpersonal Relationship Skills, Sales Skills, Social Skills and Leadership Skills. This job requires the individual to have a balanced combination of "People/Social Skills," and at the same time be "Detail Oriented" with strong follow-up skills.

Job Title: Sales Manager
Department: Loan Production
Reports to: Branch/Area Manager or Senior Management

I. Job Summary:

Hire, train, and manage the sales functions of a specific branch, area or corporate office. To achieve the outcome of maximizing quality loan production through market and loan officer development. To be knowledgeable and articulate regarding all aspects of the loan products offered such as FHA/VA, FHLMC, FNMA, JUMBO and all other Area, City, State, County and National loan programs that the company offers. To assist Loan Originators in achieving both their personal job goals as well as team and corporate goals.

II. Duties & Responsibilities:

- Recruit, hire, mentor, and manage Loan Originator staff in accordance with company and industry standards. This includes training and mentoring in areas such as product knowledge and sales training.
- Responsible for monitoring sales results and sales strategies. Responsible for monthly, quarterly, and annual budgeting for targeted sales forecast.
- Assist Loan Officers in growing their individual loan production through the development of new relationships with Realtors, builders, CPA's, financial planners, and others.
- To keep informed of trends, changes and developments in the local real estate market. To keep up with what competitors are doing. To keep up-to-date with changing rules, regulations and guidelines from FNMA, FHLMC, FHA, and VA in addition to other investors and agencies.
- To keep informed of all origination, processing, appraisal, underwriting and closing requirements for both company and investor guidelines pertaining to both government insured and privately insured mortgages.
- Negotiate price, terms and conditions with Loan Officers and mortgagors.
- Maintain a professional image and standards consistent with company policies and procedures.

III. Job Dimensions:

Directly Supervises: Loan Officers

Internal Relations: Processors, closer, supervisors, managers, and underwriters.

External Relations: Realtors and brokers, builders, developers, applicants, appraisers title companies, CPAs, financial planners, pest control companies, home inspection companies, Boards and Associations.

Other: This compensation is based on performance for not only individual performance, but also on the performance of the Loan Originators under your guidance. This is based on closed loan volume of high quality mortgage loans, which are salable on the secondary mortgage market. In addition to personal production and Loan Originator production, manager is responsible for overseeing bottom-line and profitability as well.

IV. Job Specification/Requirements:

Minimum 1 to 2 years of loan originator experience, strong sales experience and experience managing and supervising others.

Proven ability to read, write, and communicate at a level consistent with the requirements of this position and to generate independent leads for new business.

Working knowledge of standard loan products in the industry and strong familiarity with underwriting guidelines.

Must be able to work flexible hours and be willing to do some travel. Must possess a valid driver's license in the appropriate state(s).

Basic Skill Sets Required: Math Skills, Communication Skills, Interpersonal Relationship Skills, Sales Skills, Social Skills and Leadership Skills. This job requires the individual to have a balanced combination of "People/Social Skills," and at the same time be "Detail Oriented" with strong follow-up skills.

CHAPTER XIII: Building High Ethical Standards

Ethics and integrity are two words that we don't hear enough about in mortgage origination. I often hear things like, "this business draws greedy people," or "you don't see a lot of integrity in the mortgage business," or "mortgage production people have no ethics." While this is not true overall, there are bad apples in any business that can cause public perception to be negative.

There are things that we can do to change this perception that many have of the mortgage originator. It's critical to bring high ethical standards to the way you operate your business. The standards that you set for yourself, the way you stand up for yourself, and the way you communicate with your customers and clients can set you apart in the mortgage industry…especially in hiring.

Ralph Waldo Emerson said it best, "*What lies behind us and what lies before us are small matters compared to what lies within us.*" It's important to embrace this mind-set. I say mind-set because you have a choice in this matter. You have a choice to do the right thing (or the wrong thing). You have a choice to be true to yourself. Who are you? What makes you do and say things that you do and say? Why do you do and say certain things? Do you live each day by certain principles or are you making choices based on what it will give you at the moment?

Webster's dictionary defines ethics as discipline dealing with good and evil and with moral duty, principles or practice. The dictionary also defines integrity as an adherence to a code of values; incorruptibility, soundness, and completeness. For me, ethics is doing the right thing verses the wrong thing at any given moment.

It's easy to define ethics when the choices are black and white. But what about the gray areas? Even gray areas are more black and white than we think. For example, what if you receive a call from a borrower who is ready to close their loan with another lender? Their loan is approved, locked and documents are ordered. They are shopping for a better rate at the last minute and you can't offer a better rate or better fees. Do you move them to your company telling them that they are better off? No, because that would be unethical! Anytime the borrower is not better off, anytime they are not served with honesty, ethics and integrity....this is wrong. However, if you can give them spread sheets with information and advice that thy didn't have before, you may have a case for transferring the loan. The point is to make sure you are providing service that is best for them.

I don't have all the answers and I'm certainly not perfect. However, I have found that I achieve more, feel better about what I've achieved, and receive more rewards when I'm honest and ethical.

My first month in the mortgage business, I called on the top real estate broker in town and asked for the business. The Realtor told me that he had a loan that must close in two weeks. He pleaded and explained that the sellers had to move back east in two weeks and that there would be penalties if the loan didn't close within this time period. He said "I'll give you the loan only if you guarantee that you can close it within two weeks." With loan package in hand, I interviewed my manager; my processor and underwriter to have them tell me if this was possible. Because I didn't like the response I got, I took the loan back to the real estate agent the same day, gave it back to him, and told him that I felt it would have been unethical to guarantee his request, knowing that it might not be possible. I thought his jaw was going to break on the floor. He couldn't believe that he was witnessing a loan originator giving him a loan back! I didn't do that loan; however, this Realtor began to give me all of his business because he knew that I would always be honest with him. He became one of my "bread-and-butter" sources of business, because I did the right thing. Why? Because I cared more about the customer than the commission. By doing the right thing, I made more money than if I would have taken that loan and screwed it up.

So how can we bring a high level of ethics and integrity to our mortgage business? How can we hire mortgage professionals that have high ethical standards? Here are steps you can take that will set you apart to play this game at a higher, more rewarding level. Use these steps to discuss with potential candidates for hire as well as using this to train your current staff on the importance of ethics.

THINK LONG-TERM

As in my story of what happened to me as a new loan officer. I learned that it's better to tell the truth and be honest than it is to just close for the moment to receive a commission. I never forgot that and I try to always think long-term. Always think about what impact your decision will have in the future.

RAISE YOUR STANDARDS

You must decide to raise your standards to a higher level. A standard is a measure, something you set for yourself. Standards exist in every area of life and business. For example, if someone has low standards when it comes to mortgage fraud issues, they could end up in prison, if you have lower ethical standards you'll risk loss of reputation and disillusioned employees. However, if someone has high standards in these areas, their results will be consistent with the standards that they set for themselves.

Evaluate your methods of operation to determine if your firm is doing everything possible to conduct itself in an ethical manner. Review industry association code of ethics to see how you compare to their own set standards. In the area of ethics and integrity, here are a few standards that you can work on raising in your mortgage business:

STANDARDS TO EMBRACE
Honesty: My customers can count on me to tell the truth
Responsibility: My customers can count on me to communicate with them.
Honesty: My customers can count on me to honor my commitments. My word is my bond.

ESTABLISH AN ETHICS POLICY AND A BELIEF SYSTEM

It is critical that you create your own ethics policy. When you think about it, an ethics policy can't happen without a company's core belief system. What does the leadership believe about ethics? What does the production staff believe about ethics? Here are three core beliefs that you can embrace to begin developing your own ethics policy:

CORE BELIEFS TO EMBRACE
Belief One: The belief that selling is serving others, rather than taking from others.
Belief Two: The belief that you sell best when you maintain a high level of ethics and integrity.
aBelief Three: The belief that you are the best person to serve your clients and borrowers. Why...because you care more about the customer than the competition. Right?

These beliefs will carry you to the top of the mortgage origination industry. These beliefs can be the foundation of your business if you'll accept, embrace, and practice them. "Giving" will always outshine "Taking" in every category and in every measure.

Your decision to raise your standards in these areas will depend on what result you are looking for. For example, do you want to date or marry someone with low standards in the area of ethics and integrity? Do you want your doctor, lawyer, insurance agent, and car salesperson to have low standards in these areas? Do you want to work with someone who has low standards? Of course not! So let's all improve and take this to a new level by increasing the standards that we set for ourselves in these areas.

COMMUNICATE YOUR POSITION

Once your ethics policy is established, you need to communicate it to management, employees, customers and others. Build the message into your company's culture by adding your ethics policy to your recruiting packages, new hire packages, marketing materials, business cards, and flyers. Hang these up in your office. Let people know that you are committed to high standards of excellence for your customers and they can depend on you. It is also important to communicate your target for high standards both personally and in your company.

Once you commit to these types of ethical standards, you will begin to do things and say things on a daily basis that supports these standards. Hold meetings to discuss your policy with your staff. Make sure that they are aware of how important these standards are to you. If these standards are supported every day...your business will soar and you will personally feel two things: freedom and fulfillment. Working your business with high ethical standards and integrity will also help you in eliminating burnout, not a bad side benefit.

SEEK CONTINUOUS IMPROVEMENT

My customers can rely on me to seek, learn, study and keep up with my skills to serve them better. By learning more about time management, sales skills, communication skills and organizational skills, I can better serve my customer.

What does continuous education and improvement have to do with ethics? Everything. To be ethical is to have integrity. If my doctor doesn't keep up with medical advancements, then I'm not being served like I want and/or need. Remember, anytime you violate delivering the ultimate service to your customers, you compromise your value and to me, that is unethical. The cost is too high to compromise your value. There is no freedom or fulfillment for you or anyone else when you rob yourself of this. It's our responsibility, our duty to keep up on trends, new loan programs, new tools, personal skills, new technologies, and ways to serve our customers better in mortgage origination. You also need to be willing to enforce your policy. If a loan originator or processor violates your policy, are you ready to discuss or otherwise discipline them?

Do I Really Care About Serving My Customers? Answer this question. Do you care more about the commissions you'll receive, or do you care more about serving another person (the customer)? If you care more about the commissions, then you will never find the level of success, freedom, and fulfillment that can be yours by increasing the level of ethics and integrity you bring to the table.

I once met a life insurance agent who makes a little over a million dollars per year selling life insurance. I asked him how he is able to sell so much insurance. He aggressively jumped in my face and with a very serious tone he responded, *"I don't sell insurance! I provide money for people when they need it most!"* WOW! He answered my question. I knew right then and there why this insurance salesperson sells more than most. Because he cares more than most...and that caring shines through to his customers. If you can create a culture that shows your new hires how you operate your business with high ethical standards, then you're on your way to the highest level of success.

The moment you make up your mind that what you do makes a difference, it will make a difference in what you do!

DEVELOP A CULTURE OF HIGH ETHICAL STANDARDS:

✓ Checklist
Think long term and communicate this mindset to others in and around the company.
Raise your standards by reviewing your current ethical standard policy and taking it to a new level.
Establish an "Ethics Policy" in addition to a company "Belief System."
Review and embrace the "Standards" and "Beliefs" tables in this chapter.
Communicate your position through recruiting packages, new hire packages, marketing materials, business cards, flyers, etc.
Seek a continuous improvement policy. Let the world know the core values of your company and find ways to improve customer service every day.
Care for the customer. Don't get seduced with company policies that are bad for the customer. Your company's level of care will determine the level of success.

CHAPTER XIV:

✓ Master Checklist

Job Description and Plan for Hire	✓
Define job content	
Define skills, knowledge, abilities needed	
Define special market needs	
Create a plan for this hire	
Develop a timetable for each step of the plan	
Review plan	
Ask for help to solve problems encountered	
II. Sourcing for Leads	
Develop source Rolodex cards	
Develop prospect Rolodex cards	
III. Networking your Leads	
Time each day I will dedicate to networking calls	

(cont.)

(cont.)

Job Description and Plan for Hire	✓
Create note sheet for calls to candidates	
Script for this candidate meeting (fill in for each candidate)	
Create list of minimum standards each candidate must have	
IV. Interviewing and evaluating the Candidate	
Select interview selection	
Outline specific information you wish to get from this candidate; determine what you want to know that he/she hasn't told you yet	
Make notes after the interview of facts candidate has given you about background, experience, etc.	
Determine if candidate should be interviewed by any other staff members at the branch; Arrange second interviews with Area, Regional, or Senior Management if applicable	
V. Referencing for Confirmation Date Completed	
Identify at least two references, including at least one not given to you by the candidate	
Prepare script for each reference you call before you make the call	
Make notes of each reference call	
VI. Extending the Offer	
Determine that all of the candidate's questions have been answered	
Develop the job offer; prepare the compensation plan recommendation	
Obtain all necessary approvals	

Job Description and Plan for Hire	✓
Communicate offer to candidate in person	
Arrange follow-up calls to encourage candidate to accept offer	
VII. Closing the Process Date Completed	
Notify other candidates that job is filled	
Thank people in network who referred candidates	
Complete new hire paperwork	
Organize recruiting file; complete logs; retain resumes and completed applications	
Order business cards, manuals, etc.	

DEVELOP A RECRUITING PLAN AND TIME TABLE FOR THIS HIRE:

Task	Date Started	✓
Define the job, including special market needs		
Define personal skills needed		
Identify sources or leads		
Network the leads		
Interview candidates and select		
Develop list of candidates		
Conduct references		
Obtain approval for compensation plan and hire top choice		
Extend offer and get compensation		
Complete new hire paperwork		
Memorandum signed		
Loan Originator starts work		

ORDER FORM

www.MortgageSpeaker.com

Fax: (559) 323-1418 V/M: (800) 499-2242

Products	Retail	Price	S&H	TOTAL
MORTGAGE POWER (Book)	$49.95			
Loan Officer Recruiting	$39.95			
Songs of Success Volume I CD	$17.95			
Songs of Success Volume II CD	$17.95			
Mortgage Coach (software)	$695.00			
Trusted Advisor Marketing Kit	$195.00			
			TOTAL	**$**

PLEASE FILL OUT BELOW:	
Name:	VISA #:
Company:	M/C #:
Address:	American Express #:
City:	Card Expiration Date:
State/Zip Code:	Today's Date:
Work Phone:	Signature:
E-Mail:	X____________________

THANK YOU!

MIKE BAKER

V/M: (800) 499-2242 mike@mortgagespeaker.com